SANDY!

HAPPY
E. Newsl...!

It Sure Beats Working - Michel

KATE

Blue Penguin Development, Inc.
One Ash Street
Hopkinton, MA 01748 USA
508-497-0900

Email: ContactUs@BluePenguinDevelopment.com

Cover design: Barry Shuchter

www.BluePenguinDevelopment.com

ISBN: 1-4196-7065-4
ISBN-13: 978-1419670657
Library of Congress Control Number: 2007904273

Visit www.booksurge.com to order additional copies.

It Sure Beats Working

29 Quirky Stories and Practical Business
Lessons for The First-Time, Mid-Life,
Solo Professional

Michael J. Katz

2007

It Sure Beats Working

Contents

To Linda, in appreciation of your support, confidence and love.

Foreword

In late 2001, I almost pulled out what little hair I had left.

At the time, I was wrestling with the details of publishing the first issue of an e-mail newsletter, and only a few of the decisions I needed to make seemed straightforward. The strategic decisions proved toughest to make because much of the information I'd unearthed was indecipherable, at least by me.

I almost threw in the towel, but then I met Michael Katz.

Michael listened attentively to every word, even though he probably could have answered every question after the first two minutes of our conversation. And then he asked questions—insightful questions. When Michael was satisfied that he knew what I was hoping to do, he cleared the fog with ease.

I remember him saying, "Here are the three things that matter and three things that don't." Michael's advice was concrete and simple, but not simplistic. Not long after that meeting, I launched my first newsletter with confidence.

Now, Michael offers us the lessons he's learned on his journey from corporate cube dweller to successful independent professional. And if you want to know how pizza, the Marx Brothers, or a pet dog could help in your own path to entrepreneurship, read on. Michael will show you.

Michael's advice is timeless, but read it now because he hasn't yet written a book on preventing hair loss.

Michael McLaughlin
Author, *Guerrilla Marketing for Consultants*

My Own First-time, Mid-life, Solo Professional Story

I'm not going to lie to you: I never planned to start my own business. I'm not one of those guys you see on CNBC, sitting with the host, explaining how he got his start as a multi-millionaire:

> "Well, you know, Tamsen, that's an interesting question. In my case, I knew I wanted to be an entrepreneur way back in my preschool days. It was a Thursday after lunch—naptime to be exact—and the boy next to me was sound asleep on the carpet, face down in a pile of his own drool. I was inspired. I went home that night and wrote up the business plan (my mom typed it) for "Crap-azon," an online company through which I provided used, slightly soggy, industrial carpeting to third world countries. I sold that two years later in an LBO to blah, blah, blah."

No, I'm not one of those guys. In fact, if you had asked me as recently as 10 years ago if I had any plans to start my own business, I would have tossed you out of my office cube and slammed the (if it had had one) door behind you with a resounding "Ha!"

First of all, there's no entrepreneurial history in my immediate family. Well, OK, that's not exactly true. There's history, just none of it any good. My mother's father tried an assortment of ways to earn extra cash, experiments which earned him a reputation (according to my mother) as "unable to turn anything into gold." The way she tells it, simply by *touching* gold it would no longer be gold. Kind of a negative King Midas.

As for my father's father, he emigrated to this country from his native Lithuania, arriving several years ahead of his wife and offspring. After deciding to settle in New Jersey (don't ask, I don't know either), he worked in a series of factory jobs and failed ventures, including home ice delivery (slow in winter) and home coal delivery (slow in the 20th century).

My father, a very smart and observant man, who saw firsthand what the downside of entrepreneurship looked like, took his own career in the opposite direction. Not only did he have one employer his entire life, he worked in the same *building* for over 40 years. Not to take anything away from that, since by going from part-time bank teller to president of that same bank some 30+ years later, he is a walking example of the American Dream.

As for me, I took my Dad's example to heart, and went off on what seemed the obvious route: college, business school and Corporate America. Frankly, I was at first amazed to discover that anyone would pay me to do anything that didn't involve mowing their lawn; for several years, I happily put on a tie and behaved like a responsible team player.

The truth is, I'm quite sure I'd still be there today, were it not for the convergence of a number of factors.

First of all, I was lured by the call of the Internet. In the late nineties, any job-related fear that was floating around in the business world wasn't about too *little* security, it was about being the only one to miss out on making a ton of money and retiring early from some dot com bonanza. I personally knew several people who had founded or gone to work at dot coms and who, in a matter of months, were rolling in cash.

Second, I was getting close to 40. I wasn't concerned about getting old so much as realizing that things were just too predictable in my daily work life. The way I look at it, working for someone else (particularly when it's a large company) is like living with your parents: you'll never starve, but you'll frequently be bored to tears. Sitting in meeting after endless meeting, I got to the point where I would sometimes toy with the idea of taking my own life, rather than listen to one more of my co-workers "play devil's advocate" with respect to an idea that, even if implemented, would make little difference to anyone.

And finally, at some point it dawned on me that I wasn't going far beyond the ranks of middle management. In a world where sheer brain power is the most important yardstick for success, I'm just another face in the crowd. I was aware that I was *funnier* than most businesspeople, but being funny in a typical corporate environment is like being an extremely tall baseball player—unusual and occasionally oddly useful, but more of an interesting diversion than anything else. My boss frequently told me I had "missed my calling," which, if you think about it, is a nice compliment from just about anybody *except* your boss.

So, somehow, with a vague business idea in mind, a bunch of factors beginning to brew the Michael-Katz-must-start-his-own-company perfect storm, and a spoken commitment to myself, my family and my friends that "I'm not turning 40 in that place," I decided that when the upcoming acquisition of my then-employer was complete, I would take that as my signal to leave.

The acquisition kept getting delayed and delayed, until finally, one day, it happened. My boss walked into our weekly staff meeting and announced, "The deal closed this morning." I was two months shy of my 40th birthday; I gave my notice the next day.

Why I Wrote This Book for You

So much of what is written about entrepreneurship in this country suggests that "you've either got it or you don't." Like star athletes who stand out from the pack at a very early age, if you're not a Mark Cuban (who sold garbage bags door-to-door when he was 12) or a Ross Perot (who, legend has it, delivered newspapers on horseback when he was a kid), it's easy to believe that if you haven't sailed your self-employment ship by the time you're 25 or so, it's long ago left port, and your only career option is to work for someone else.

I'm here to tell you—*this book is here to tell you*—that it's not true. Sure, there are people who were cut out from the start to work on their own. But that's only one path. For many of us—the people I like to think of as "reluctant entrepreneurs"—self-employment is more of a gradual awakening; a number of factors that slowly add up to a decision to go off and try something new.

The purpose of this book, therefore, is threefold:

- To encourage you to build a work life that is everything you want it to be.
- To offer some experience-based suggestions and perspective on how to create that life.
- To reassure you that you—and I do mean you—can make it on your own, if that's what you want.

In the end, starting your own business is not always easy and not always fun. But, as I like to say, it sure beats working.

Here's to your professional success and, more importantly, to your happiness.

Michael Katz
Hopkinton, Massachusetts
June 14, 2007

How to Use This Book

Short answer: Any way you like.

Longer answer: This isn't a regular business book. For one thing, it's funny. In fact, it may even be funnier than it is useful. What I've discovered, however, is that many people learn and enjoy more by having their "useful information" mixed in with entertainment (if you're not one of these people, please return this book neatly to the shelf).

Second, it's divided into 29 short, distinct, stand-alone stories, each intended to demonstrate a particular insight in building a business as a solo professional. I doubt you'd want to read them all at once. My intention instead is to give you an inspiring collection of tasty hors d'oeuvres, rather than a single, big meal. So feel free to jump around and read them out of sequence—an order which, I confess, is largely arbitrary anyway.

Seven turns on the highway,
Seven rivers to cross.
Sometimes, you feel like you could fly away,
Sometimes, you get lost.

And sometimes, in the darkened night,
You see the crossroad sign.
One way is the morning light,
You got to make up your mind.

Somebody's calling your name.

"Seven Turns"
Allman Brothers Band

Lesson #1

Declare Yourself a Competent Professional

A few years ago, my family and I spent the last days of our summer vacation with friends in Northampton, Massachusetts, a little town located about 100 miles west of Boston.

Northampton is a funky, artsy kind of place, and in the evening during the summer you can hardly open your car door without banging into one of the many street performers set up on the sidewalk (I know, because I did).

It's a fun atmosphere, and after watching these folks for a couple of days, I half-jokingly suggested to my then 11-year-old son Evan that he could probably do pretty well if he stood out there one night and did some of his juggling. To my surprise, he took me up on it, and so that very evening (with the rest of the family cleverly pretending we didn't know him), Evan found a spot in front of an art gallery, dropped his baseball cap upside down on the ground and went to work.

To my complete shock, somebody threw a handful of change into his hat within about 15 seconds. A minute later, someone else dropped in a dollar bill. A few more minutes, a few more dollars. He did so well, in fact, over the next 30 minutes, that I began wondering if maybe juggling was a better career path than consulting.

Then something really interesting happened. One of the spectators asked him, "How long have you been a professional?" Evan launched into a humble explanation of how he really wasn't a professional, and that he still had a long way to go. The man just smiled and said, "Kid, if you're earning money, you're a professional."

As we walked back to our car that night, it occurred to me that Evan had learned an important lesson about running his own business: Performing on the street is a great way to avoid paying income tax.

No, ha, ha, I am of course just kidding. What he learned was that when you work on your own, you become "certified" as a professional as soon as somebody is willing to pay you. No university or company or governing body is going to show up one day and tell you that you've earned the right to set up a business doing whatever it is you do. You simply have to claim it for yourself.

Interestingly, I've discovered that a tendency to view oneself as "not yet good enough" is not the exclusive realm of 6th grade jugglers.

I had lunch recently with my friend Jennifer, a few weeks after she decided to take the plunge and set herself up as a business consultant. If you were to take out a blank sheet of paper and write down the ideal qualifications for a consultant in Jennifer's industry, you'd end up describing her: fifteen years of industry-specific experience; ability to spot trends before other people; Harvard MBA; great with numbers; articulate speaker; common sense; reliable; friendly; etc.

She had every possible box checked, and yet when we had lunch that day, guess what was holding her back: doubts about her own qualifications.

I can assure you that Jennifer is not the exception. I get frequent invitations to share coffee with friends, colleagues and others who have left or are considering leaving the corporate world, and who want to talk with someone who has already made the leap. The one thing they tend to have in common—regardless of what their credentials might be—is that most people just starting out question their right to call themselves "expert."

Maybe you're reading this as you consider your own new career as a solo professional. If so, I'd like to offer you the same advice I offer everybody who joins me for that cup of coffee (and, in the process, maybe save you six months of mental anguish): You're good enough to call yourself a professional at whatever it is you do. I guarantee it.

Whatever obstacles might arise between where you are and where you want to go, your skill level is not going to be one of them. People don't hire professionals based on an objective evaluation of their skills.

Do you really have any idea how *technically* capable your attorney is? Are the *medical skills* of your doctor better or worse than those of the guy down the street? Who knows?! The fact is, unless you're on trial for murder, or awaiting a heart transplant, it really doesn't matter. Prospective clients know that most professionals in a given field can get the job done just fine.

When it comes to growing your business, therefore, you needn't worry about being good enough (you already are). Your attention should be on sharpening your focus, gaining visibility, differentiating your services and learning how to persuade people that you can do something to help them fix their problems.

Whatever you do, don't waste any more precious time waiting for someone to show up and give you permission to call yourself an expert. Write your newsletters, give your speeches, share your opinions and do your juggling as the industry-leading professional that you are, and it will be true.

Lesson #2

Bill Flat Fee If You Want to Make a Lot of Money

If you've never experienced Halloween firsthand, I encourage you to plan a trip to the U.S. for next October. Of all the holidays, it's my favorite. Not just because I get to roam around the neighborhood in a terrifying costume (this year, I went as a creepy, middle-aged white guy), but because for one day each year, you and your children have permission to walk down any driveway, ring any doorbell and invite yourselves into the homes of people you've never met.

As a parent, however, there is one downside: sugar intake regulation. The kids come home with tons of candy, and some ground rules need to be established.

In previous years, my wife Linda and I went with the ever-popular "one piece per day" rule. That worked when the kids were little, since they didn't count so well. Between Daddy eating some and Mommy throwing some in the garbage, nobody on the Kids Team ever thought to wonder why it was all gone by Thanksgiving.

Today, however, the one-a-day rule doesn't work. Not only have the kids gotten more efficient at rounding up the treats (385 pieces collectively this year), they've instituted rigid inventory controls that make it impossible for us to surreptitiously drain the supply (I think they're using the Dewey Decimal System). If we stuck with the one-a-day rule, they'd still be eating it by the *next* time the Red Sox win the World Series.

So this year, we came up with a new concept: "All you can eat for one week." That's right, for seven days, they can have as much candy as they want, with the understanding that come Day 8, we go back to "normal."

Guess what? It worked out pretty well. The kids got to decide how much is enough; we didn't have to keep track of who had what each day; and the entire thing was over in a week.

Believe it or not, the candy idea was inspired by the approach I use for setting my coaching and consulting fees. If you're thinking of charging clients on an hourly basis (i.e. you're counting each piece of candy), I encourage you to consider this approach instead.

In my case, all-you-can-eat pricing means that whether I'm developing a newsletter for a client or coaching someone through doing it herself, I no longer tie the fee to the time involved. Instead, my price is based on the length of the engagement (e.g. three months) or the result itself (e.g. E-Newsletter up and running). In either case, there is no pre-defined limit on how much or how often we interact.

I've played around with a bunch of different pricing models over the years, but this one is the best by far. Here's why:

- **It's better for my clients.** Back in the days when I charged by the hour, I found that many clients would literally call me up and talk as fast as possible, to minimize their cost. For the same reason, others thought twice about picking up the phone when they had a simple question. As a result, the calls were less productive (because I didn't get as much detailed, thoughtful information from them) and less enjoyable (because we spent very little time on non-business topics).

Today, with no clock ticking away in the background, I have conversations with clients that are more relaxed and more personal, and as a result, I find that they're more likely to involve me in multiple aspects of their business. I've even found that the extra time spent on non-business tangents gives me greater insight into who my clients are, allowing me to do a better job of serving them.

- **It's better for me.** According to rock-and-roll folklore, Keith Richards of the Rolling Stones wrote the group's megahit "Satisfaction" in 20 minutes, after hearing it in a dream the night before. I have no idea how much that song has been worth to him over the years, but I think it's safe to say that if Mick had been paying him by the hour, he'd have earned quite a bit less. Likewise, as a professional, linking your fee to time spent limits your compensation, and doesn't correlate with what your clients really care about anyway: results.

   I also love the fact that fixed-fee billing has liberated me from having to track my time in 15-minute increments. And now when I work on a client idea while running or driving or mowing the lawn, I don't have to wrestle with the question of how to bill for it.

But I know what you're thinking. "What about the

clients who call you every day and take advantage of the arrangement? Doesn't that destroy the all-you-can-eat model?"

You know what? It never happens. They've all got businesses to run and have no more interest in wasting time than I do (in fact, probably less, since I really enjoy wasting time). Sure, there are those who call more frequently than others, but like a restaurant that offers all-you-can-eat service, some people cost more, some people cost less, and it all just balances out in the end.

If you're just starting out as a professional or are unhappy with the constraints of hourly fees, give the all-you-can-eat approach some consideration. If my experience is any indication, taking the clock out of the equation will improve the nature of your client relationships, and have no negative impact on your compensation.

And by the way, if you know anybody who could use about 15 pounds of slightly handled candy, please let me know.

Lesson #3

Narrow Your Focus

I'm not going to lie to you: I'm feeling pretty disappointed right now. *People Magazine* just came out with its list of the "50 Most Beautiful People in the World" and, once again, my name was nowhere to be found.

Now to some people (by which I mean the people who have actually seen what I look like), this may not come as a surprise. After all, I'm sure you'd say, this list is heavily biased towards actors, musicians and professional athletes, and with a few hundred million people to choose from in this country alone, it shouldn't be too big of a surprise to learn that I was overlooked by the "researchers" at *People*.

But what if they narrowed the parameters of the list? What if, instead of looking for the "50 Most Beautiful People in the *World*," they looked for the "50 Most Beautiful People in Massachusetts?" I'd certainly do a lot better, although I admit, I still wouldn't make the cut.

How about the "50 Most Beautiful Middle-aged Men in Eastern Massachusetts?" Still better.

I think you can see what I'm getting at. While I could certainly improve my chances at the *World* Top 50 by eating better, working out more often, getting (extensive) cosmetic surgery, becoming a professional athlete, etc., the most efficient way to become a winner is simply to *narrow the scope of the contest*.

Think about this: Let's say you're a financial planner whose business provides financial planning services in general. I think you'd agree that it's going to be a pretty tough slog to try to stand out from the thousands of other financial planners out there who offer essentially the same services.

Now, just for fun, let's say instead that you decide to *narrow* your focus and offer financial planning advice to one group only—female small business owners in the southwestern United States. In this second example, while you'd certainly have a (much) smaller market of potential clients, *among the people in this segment, you'd have a significantly easier time standing out and being remembered.*

Why? Two reasons. First, because you won't have much (if any) direct competition. As one of a handful of people who exclusively serve female small business owners in the southwestern United States, you'd always be on the short list of financial planners to consider whenever a member of this audience went in search of advice.

Second, those who meet you—based solely on the fact that you specialize—will naturally assume that you are an expert. For example, who do you think knows more about pizza: the owner of "Mike's Restaurant" or the owner of "Joe's World of Nothing But Pizza?" Don't you assume it's Joe?

The fact is, Joe could have decided yesterday to focus his business on pizza, and may possess no more pizza knowledge than Mike. But when you learn of a specialty, you assume expertise comes with it.

Granted, if you *over*-niche your business you'll be in danger of having too small a target audience. Being king of a market with one person in it won't do you much good.

In my experience, however, most professionals—the attorneys offering legal services, the life coaches helping people live better lives, the consultants selling leadership training—are nowhere near becoming *too* focused. Instead, they are way at the other end of the spectrum, bumping up against each other in the competition to be one of the "50 Most Beautiful _____ in the World."

I recognize that this may at first seem a bit counterintuitive. Doesn't a broader focus give me more potential clients? Absolutely. The problem is that you don't want *potential* clients, you want actual clients (since they tend to be the ones who pay you *actual* money). And if you insist on staking out too broad a topic area, you'll never make it onto anybody's radar screen.

There's a lot of noise out there, and you don't have the marketing budget needed to simply blast your way through it. And so while I encourage you to make your business the best it can be, don't overlook an important piece of the puzzle: finding a pond without many fish in it.

Now if you'll excuse me, I'm off to see if I can convince the editors of *People* to run an issue on "The 50 Most Beautiful Bald, Ambidextrous, Middle-aged Men Named Michael in Eastern Massachusetts." In that pond, I may in fact have a chance.

Lesson #4

Humanize Your Interactions

I was half-watching the 11 o'clock news the other night, jumping around among the three local networks. It was amazing to see how similar the programs were: same stories, same sound bites, same "Live from the scene of..." segments. Most times, they even covered the news in the same *order* (is there an FCC regulation that requires sports to come on at 20 minutes past the hour?).

It suddenly dawned on me that the primary difference— and, therefore, the determining factor between who's #1 and who isn't—isn't the product itself (i.e. the news). It's the extra stuff: the banter and chitchat and "How about that heat wave?" side conversations that go on in-between the real stories. Take that out, and it's all the same.

I mention this because one question that often comes up relating to developing web sites, newsletters or other marketing collateral content is, "Should we include any 'non-business stuff,' and if so, how much?"

Okay, that's two questions, but stay with me. Answer number one is, "Yes." Answer number two is, "Sprinkle it lightly."

Two reasons to include this "soft stuff:"

- **Human beings have short attention spans.** Blame it on MTV, blame it on public schools, blame it on breakfast cereal with 17% sugar content. Whatever you attribute it to, it's a fact that in today's world, most people can't stick with one topic for very long (you still with me?).

And so just as the networks deliberately inject conversation in-between the real news to give you a break, your message will get through most effectively when you also throw in some tidbits that are not necessarily about the business at hand.

- **Effective company communications show the people *behind* the business, not just the business itself.** It's no coincidence that President Bush frequently walks up to press conference microphones having just finished exercising, or with his dogs in tow, or with some kind of ranching gizmo in his hand. It's all done as part of a conscious attempt to shine a light on his human side, so that viewers will be more willing to "buy" his message. (I know what you're thinking: Maybe they should get the *Vice* President a couple of dogs.)

   Likewise, when you include a restaurant or book review in your newsletter; show photos of actual employees who actually work for your actual company on your web site; or talk about a charity event in which you recently participated as a lead-in to a group presentation, you help your audience make a connection with you and your company that transcends whatever product or service you have to offer.

In terms of how much to do this, I say "sprinkle lightly" because you don't want the filler to dominate. Although the news show banter may indeed be the differentiator, it's safe to assume that if that's all there were, nobody would watch at all.

Humanizing your interactions with customers and prospects is what makes doing business with you enjoyable. And like it or not, people do business with people they like. Useful information does not have to be dry and serious, and the more you can cut up the meat, the easier it is to digest.

Lesson #5

Don't Sell Your Reputation

When I was a kid, I loved watching the old Marx Brothers movies. This was way before VCRs or cable TV, of course, and with only a handful of channels to choose from, we ended up watching the same films over and over again. One in particular, "Go West" (1940), has a train scene which is now a classic.

Running out of coal and faced with a deadline, the brothers decide to start chopping up the train itself to use for fuel. The plan works, although when they finally limp into their destination, laughing and cheering, there's not much left of the train except the wheels and engine. Not exactly what you would call a long-term transportation solution.

And yet today, over 65 years later, the Marx Brothers' strategic planning philosophy is alive and well in many businesses.

Consider, for example, my experience the other day at a local café (no, it wasn't a Starbucks, but same idea). Everything was perfect: classical music, leafy plants, comfy chairs and a great coffee smell in the air, all wrapped together to create an experience that said, "Today, I'm going to treat myself to something special."

All went well until they actually handed me my coffee. Wrapped around the paper cup, obscuring the café's logo, was a piece of cardboard with an ad printed on it for an unrelated business.

Hello? What are these people thinking? In the blink of an eye, that ad broke the fragile spell that let me rationalize paying $1.65 for a 10-ounce cup of coffee. It diminished my overall experience with the business.

After all the dollars spent creating the perfect style and atmosphere, after all the effort expended to train staff on how to properly manage the store and produce the perfect cup of coffee, somebody at that company decided there were a few extra dollars to be made by selling ad space on the coffee cups. In the process, they put their entire business model at risk.

Like the Marx Brothers, these guys are chopping up the train for fuel; they're selling off the asset they've built, one paper cup at a time.

The online version of this same approach occurs in relation to affiliate programs. If you're not familiar with the term, affiliate programs refer to payment plans whereby a company pays a commission to somebody else in exchange for referring leads. You may have seen this, for example, with Amazon, which pays web sites a percentage of the sales that come from books that are promoted on those web sites and then linked to (and ultimately purchased on) Amazon.

Don't get me wrong—this is a great arrangement, and I'm involved in several myself. But here's the problem: There's a huge potential for a conflict of interest. If I get a piece of every book or video or product that I tell you about, it doesn't take long for me to realize that the stronger a recommendation I make to you, the more money I stand to make. That's a problem.

A couple of months ago, I asked an industry expert to review one of my products, in the hope that she would like it and tell her readers about it. She was happy to do it, although it vaguely occurred to me during our conversation that she was much more interested in discussing—and negotiating—the size of her commission, than in talking about the product itself. Sure enough, when her review came out, it was glowing.

Sure, I was thrilled about the review and the sales it ultimately brought. However, over the next several weeks, as I read glowing review after glowing review of other products in her newsletter, I realized that she wasn't "reviewing" products—i.e. telling me which were good and which were bad—she was simply promoting products in the hope of earning a commission.

Why is this a problem? Back to the Marx Brothers. If you've developed a loyal following, whether through your newsletter, articles or general reputation in the community, people naturally want to know what you think. That's good; they respect your opinion. The worst thing you can do, however, is mortgage this reputation in exchange for a few dollars. Once people realize that your opinion is for sale, and that your recommendations are not worth anything, you'll have no more reputation, no more affiliate fees and, worst of all, an inability to sell whatever it is you really do (I'm assuming you're not making your living off of these fees).

If you want to be part of affiliate programs, that's fine. Just make sure that when you recommend something, people know you're being compensated. Even better, only recommend those things that you truly use, love and would recommend anyway.

As a small business owner in particular, with little or no marketing budget, your reputation is by far the most important source of your continued success. Learn from Groucho's mistake: If you're in it for the long haul, you're going to need your train for more than just one ride.

Lesson #6

Believe in Yourself

"Millionaires don't believe in astrology. Billionaires do."
—Andrew Carnegie (1835-1919)

My son Evan has been involved in karate since he was about six years old. He's taken lessons at several different schools over the years as we've moved, schools have closed, or his interests have changed.

When he was about 10, the school he was studying with at the time announced that there was a special "Board Breaking Class" coming up. Although I don't know many people who have ever actually been attacked by a board, his instructor thought it would be good for the kids to put some of their skills to the test. So we signed up.

We got there early, and Evan ran right over to pick up his allotted ten pieces of one-foot square, one-inch thick pine. After a brief demonstration by the instructor (who apparently was using trick wood, based on the way it crumbled with just the slightest touch of his hand), Evan got in line with the other kids.

One by one they broke the wood, and I have to admit that by the time it came to Evan's turn, I was as excited as he was. He walked over, knelt down, positioned the wood between the two cinder blocks provided, and raised his hand high over his head. Then, with one quick, focused movement, he brought his hand down on the wood as hard as he could.

Nothing happened. The wood just sat there looking at him. So he tried it again. Nothing. And again, and again, AND AGAIN. Nothing, nothing, NOTHING. From 20 feet away I could see how red his hand was getting, and I finally had to stop him so he wouldn't hurt himself. Needless to say, we went home that night very disappointed.

Later that weekend, and now wondering what to do with ten pieces of one-foot square, one-inch thick pine, I set the wood up in the basement between two cinder blocks. Then I went upstairs to find Evan.

Once again, he knelt down, raised his hand and brought his fist down on the wood. This time, however, BOOM! The wood snapped in half as his hand reached the floor. After a quick celebration filled with the usual idiotic hooting and hollering we American males are famous for, I put another board down for him to break. Boom, broken. And another, same thing. He broke five boards in a row in about two minutes, and I suddenly began fearing for the lives of all the cutting boards in our kitchen.

You know the point of the story. When you believe that you can do something, it's easy. When you don't, it's impossible.

One of the biggest obstacles standing in the way of first time entrepreneurs is belief. Metaphorically speaking, "your board hasn't broken yet," and since you have no historical evidence to suggest that it ever will, you wonder if maybe you should just take your wood and go home (i.e. get a "real job").

This next part is important, so pay attention. Like you, I never imagined I'd be running my own business, and like you, when I first started out, I spent many days, weeks and months wondering if I had what it takes. I realize now how much time I wasted and how much worry I put myself through, simply because I didn't realize that I always had it.

So let me save you months of agony and tell you right now that YOU ARE GOOD ENOUGH. That's a fact. The only thing standing in your way is your own faith in yourself.

By the way, I'm well aware that there are people who would argue that words like "faith" and "belief" aren't measurable or tangible enough to deserve a place in serious business. I disagree, and Evan and I are willing to bet that none of those people have ever broken a piece of wood with their bare hands.

Lesson #7

Stop Trying to Sell

I remember it as if it were yesterday. I got home from my office, and my wife Linda told me in no uncertain terms that I had to go sleep on the family room couch. Not only that, but for the next two nights in a row, she did it again.

Don't worry, it's not what you think. What happened was, we had adopted a dog (a two-year-old beauty named Abbie), and I slept next to her for a few nights to keep her company.

Knowing that a new dog was coming soon, I had made a call the week before to a company that sells invisible fencing, a system that keeps a dog on the property via an electronic collar. We set up an appointment, and a couple of days later, a woman named Marie showed up at the house.

From her big smile as she stepped out of her car, to her clear interest in talking about me rather than just her company, to the fistful of invisible fence ground flags that she presumptively handed over as she stepped in the back door, I knew right away that I was dealing with a pro.

But even then, it was only after she had left that I realized just how skilled she was. Because, despite my not having been ready to buy when she arrived, after we spent an hour or so talking about the weather, my kids, my house and (of course) her product, she walked out with a sale. And, interestingly enough, I never once felt pressured.

Think about what she accomplished. She arrived stone cold at the home of a prospect (Marie was not even who I spoke with on the phone) and was immediately faced with having to build rapport and close the sale *simultaneously*. Not an easy thing to do. Spend too much time on rapport and risk going home with a new friend, but no sale. Push too hard on selling and risk having me walk away. It's a thin line to walk, and only a real sales expert can do it consistently.

I don't mind telling you that I'm not one of those experts, and frankly, I couldn't walk that line if it were a mile wide and painted on the ground in bright red. By the time I get to the point of closing a sale, I need months (not minutes) of rapport-building history to compensate for my selling ineptitude.

The good news here is that you don't need to build rapport and close the sale at the same time. I've got nothing but respect and awe for the Maries of the world who can; but if, like me and many other professionals, you find yourself challenged in this area, it's perfectly effective to separate the two events.

With that in mind, I offer three suggestions:

- **DON'T wait until you need the sale.** If the only time I hear from you is when you are trying to close me, or when you want me to give you some referrals, you're going to have an uphill battle. You don't need a dog's nose to smell the, "guy-who-just-finished-a-project-and-is-desperate-for-the-next-one" from a mile away.

  If, on the other hand, you work to stay in touch with your network just for the sake of staying in touch, you'll find it easier and more natural to shift into selling mode when the opportunity arises with one of these people.

- **DO be systematic.** Whether it's white papers you distribute, colleagues you call/e-mail, business meetings you attend, E-Newsletters you write, or some combination, you need to schedule these events into your calendar. In my experience, if you don't have a specific relationship communications plan (hint: if it's not on paper, you don't have one), this kind of thing becomes the walking definition of "back burner:" You'll never get around to doing it.

- **DON'T apply the filter too tightly.** If, like Marie, you're making sales calls today with the intention of closing sales today, it makes sense to try and figure out who the hot prospects are now. Long-term rapport building, however, takes the opposite approach—staying in touch with lots of people over a long period of time, knowing that any one of them could ultimately be (or lead you to) a sale. When you're that far back in the chain of events that need to take place, it's hard to predict who is ultimately going to lead you to the promised land. So stay in touch with a lot of people, not just the ones who seem likely to bring you something today.

A true story:

A recent client project came about as a result of my sending a congratulatory e-mail to the founder of a local company, after seeing him profiled in a weekly business paper. He and I had spoken briefly about six months earlier, he'd been getting my newsletter ever since, and I just thought I'd say hello.

Ten minutes after he got my e-mail, he called. We met the next week, and before I even had a chance to go back to my office and write up a proposal, he and his partner had e-mailed to hire me.

Was it a fast sale? I suppose so. But the only reason it happened so fast and the meeting went so well was because by the time I walked in the door, we already had a long term relationship. The rest was just working out the details.

One way or the other, you've got to close sales to make money. And the way I see it, that means you've got two options: You can either get really good at selling, or you can build connections that are so strong, the closing takes care of itself. Woof, woof!

Lesson #8

Become the Leading Expert in Something

The first time I met Rosalind Joffe, she introduced herself to me as a "leadership coach," someone who took people from "where they are to where they want to be."

Several months later, when she hired me to help her with her E-Newsletter, we sat down together and began talking about her business. In the course of our conversation, she told me she lived with both Multiple Sclerosis (25 years) and Ulcerative Colitis (12 years). I filed away these two facts as interesting, but irrelevant, and we spent the next couple of months working on her newsletter.

Frankly, her focus at the time wasn't all that distinctive. Here in Boston, you run into a ton of life and leadership coaches, and I don't mind telling you that we were having a tough time finding an angle or topic area for her newsletter that would break through the e-mail clutter and set her apart from the pack.

Then one day, the light came on. Although Rosalind's business was focused on helping businesspeople become better leaders, she spent a lot of time "on the side" helping other people with chronic illness learn how to cope (and thrive) in the workplace.

After all, in the 25 years since she was first diagnosed with MS, she had raised a family, started her own business and pretty much figured out the ins and outs of how to be successful no matter what your health. The fact is, if you suddenly found yourself in a similar situation, she's exactly the person you'd want to talk to.

One brief phone call later, we decided to refocus Rosalind's entire business—not just her newsletter—ultimately rebranding it as "CICoach: thriving in the workplace while living with chronic illness."

The result? I'm so glad you asked. Within six months, Rosalind's profile skyrocketed; she was quoted in the *Wall Street Journal* (front page) and interviewed on the radio by Sam Donaldson. Her coaching business took off as she gained national prominence as a spokesperson for, and advisor to, people who live with chronic illness and who want to continue working productively.

Here's the point: Rosalind's tremendous success is a good example of the traction you get by specializing in one thing. When a *Wall Street Journal* reporter went looking for somebody who could speak on the topic of "chronic illness in the workplace," it didn't take her long to find Rosalind.

But that's only part of what's happening here. Not only is Rosalind specializing, she's managed to take a personal experience (i.e. 25 years living with chronic illness) and convert it from something that was at best a *neutral* aspect of her business and turn it into her single most distinctive credential.

Think about that for a minute. *Any* leadership coach could decide tomorrow to narrow his focus to chronic illness in the workplace. Rosalind, however, has lived it.

Given the choice between Rosalind and somebody who simply specializes in this area, who would you rather have for a coach? She's taken a life experience most people would consider an obstacle and turned it into her primary competitive advantage. Wow.

So here's my question for you: What unique life experience or personal trait of *yours* can be converted from a liability into a business advantage?

As for me, I'm now focused on finding a way to leverage rampant baldness.

Lesson #9

Give People a Reason to Spread the Word About You

Arriving home from my office one day several years ago, my then 3-year-old son Jonathan attacked me at the door. According to scientific research he had been conducting that morning in preschool, "The bees buzz from flower to flower to make the garden pretty."

I'm no entomologist, but that seemed about right, so I thanked him for bringing me up to speed.

Later that night, however, his older brother Evan set me straight. According to Evan (who at the time was a highly regarded bug expert in his own right, in the Hopkinton, Massachusetts, 4th grade), the bees don't go from flower to flower "to make the garden pretty." No, he insisted, they couldn't care less about making the flowers grow.

They go from flower to flower because they want nectar, and in the process of slurping it up (or whatever), flower pollen gets caught on their sticky little bee legs. When they move on to the next flower (again, for the nectar), some of the pollen drops off their legs, and pollination occurs.

His point was simple. The growth of your garden is a fortunate, but unintentional side effect of a bee's selfish desire for nectar.

Believe it or not, this is directly related to one of the marketing questions I hear most: "How can I generate word-of-mouth interest in my business?"

Here's what I mean. One of the great things about modern communications technology (e-mail, instant messaging, cell phones, etc.) is that it's easy to instantly share information with others. Gone are the days when you had to photocopy an article and stuff it in an envelope if you thought it might be of interest to somebody else. Today, you just paste it, link it or forward it along.

This so-called "viral effect" isn't a new concept. Many businesspeople do things to encourage their network of friends, family, colleagues and clients to pass the word. Examples include displaying prominent "Click here to forward" buttons in newsletters, sending special company announcements in e-mails, or mailing multiple fridge magnets to customers.

All good stuff. The disconnect is that most people apply these tactics without any consideration for the motivation of *the bee.*

In other words, encouraging me to spread the word about your business is very much like encouraging the bee community to go pollinate some flowers. Unless there's nectar in it for me, I'm not going to be all that interested.

In the case of information about your business, the nectar is useful content.

Recipients of your communications will only share them with *their* friends, *their* clients and *their* colleagues if the content itself is valuable. If they can help (or impress) people they know by forwarding a valuable piece of information, or letting someone know about a great resource for topic X, they'll do it.

On the other hand, asking them to forward something along simply to help you out—or even worse, to forward a blatant advertisement for your services—is an uphill climb.

And so from a viral marketing standpoint, the most effective communications you can produce are those that are valuable in and of themselves. White papers, electronic newsletters, tips, guidelines, whatever—if it's something of value to me, I *may* share it with my network (and, in the process, share you with them). Anything short of that, and you'll have a tough time generating buzz (sorry) with people who are busily trying to live their lives.

Lesson #10

Give Away Free, Useful Information

Around the house, my wife Linda and I have fairly well-defined job assignments. Some are based on personal preference (I handle the finances), some on competency (she manages our trips and vacations), and some are completely arbitrary (I kill insects; she does laundry).

A few jobs, however, are shared between us, more or less equally. Among these, unfortunately, is meal preparation.

I say unfortunately, because there are times—last night for example—when neither one of us feels like (or is willing to start) cooking anything. On nights like this we resort to takeout, so at 5:45 p.m. yesterday afternoon, I found myself pulling into the parking lot of a local Thai restaurant.

In the interest of full disclosure, calling this place a "restaurant" is like calling the stuff on top of my head "hair." Technically accurate, perhaps, but laughable when compared with other, more impressive structures. The entire place is maybe 25 feet wide, with room for about ten people. Even the kitchen, completely in view behind a small counter and cash register, is bigger than the seating area.

I arrived 10 minutes early, so I took a seat in one of the chairs by the front counter. I had been there about two minutes when I noticed an old man with a white apron coming out of the kitchen, carrying something in his hands. He walked up to me, bowed and handed me what turned out to be a cup of tea. And then he turned and walked away.

I couldn't help thinking that this was a perfectly executed customer service experience. Not because the tea was so wonderful, but because it came about in an unexpected way. Not in response to a request on my part, not as an apology for keeping me waiting (I was early), not because there was a big sign in the window declaring that Wednesday was "complimentary tea day." Just a nice gesture from a man who saw me waiting and wanted to make me feel at home.

Needless to say, despite the modest surroundings, this place instantly became my favorite local restaurant.

So, I'm sure you're wondering, how can you apply this "give your customers an unexpected gift" concept to your business, so that you can also have people thinking warm and fuzzy thoughts about you?

Easy: Hire an old man to bring them tea. No, ha, ha, I am of course just kidding. Give away something unexpected and valuable when you first come in contact with a new colleague. This could be somebody you met the night before at a business event, somebody who's just signed up for your E-Newsletter or even a prospective client, as a follow-up to a meeting. Here's how you do it in two easy steps:

- Write a brief information piece related to your area of expertise. A top 10 list of suggestions, an analysis of data in your industry, a how-to document of some kind. It doesn't matter what, as long as it's arguably valuable and within the scope of whatever it is you do. To save yourself some effort, pick a topic that won't get old very fast, so you don't have to keep updating it.

- Send the document to people as a follow-up to meeting them (hard copy on your letterhead through regular mail is worth the extra effort for those people who you feel warrant it).

That's it. A low-cost, unexpected bit of value for your newfound friends.

Does it make up for inferior service or low quality work? Of course not. No more than a cup of tea makes up for poor quality food. But—and this is the key here—in a world where your clients and prospective clients have many options to choose from, where even the deals and bonuses offered by most companies have more strings attached than a parade balloon on Thanksgiving Day, simple, human, unexpected gestures go a long way.

Lesson #11

Clearly and Simply State What You Do

For reasons I frankly can't remember, I volunteered to coach my son Evan's basketball team this year. It's not a huge time commitment, however as someone whose involvement with organized basketball (i.e. referees, scoreboards, fans) came to a screeching halt midway through the Carter administration, I found myself scrambling in the first few weeks, trying to pull things together.

One of my responsibilities as coach involves communicating with the parents. One day, after a brief e-mail exchange regarding an upcoming game, I received a question from one of the moms, apparently in response to my e-mail signature listing my job title as "Chief Penguin." Here's what she said:

"I just have to ask…What exactly does a Chief Penguin do? Sounds fresh, but I was wondering what your company does."

First of all, you'll be proud to know I resisted the temptation to tell her that a Chief Penguin does whatever the hell he wants.

It did get me thinking, however. Because having a good answer to the "What does your company do?" question is both important and challenging.

It's important because if you believe in the power of word-of-mouth as a way to grow your business, it's in your best interest to take advantage of every opportunity that arises to spread the word. When somebody actually *asks* the question, you want to be ready.

It's challenging, however, because unless you give the other person something that can be both understood and remembered (more or less), they'll never be able to carry your message to the next person.

For a long time, I thought I had this problem solved with my "elevator statement." If you're not familiar with this concept, it refers to a short, pithy summary of a person or business, so named because you're supposed to be able to spit one out in the time it takes to ride in an elevator.

What I eventually decided, however, was that my pat, highly polished statement was both hard to understand and too slick for the recipient to hold onto. Like wedding china, it was the kind of thing I would trot out of the cabinet whenever company came over, but as a practical matter, it wasn't quite right for everyday use.

The thing is, most of the word-of-mouth-ish opportunities that arise in my life (and, I'm willing to bet, in yours) are not formal ones. They happen at the supermarket, or at the movie theater, or when somebody's mother asks, "What exactly does a Chief Penguin do?"

And so with that in mind, I encourage you to get going on your best word-of-mouth foot by developing a more conversational description of your business. Here are some specific suggestions for doing that:

- **Lose the jargon.** Telling your next door neighbor that your company is "the leading provider of cross-promulgated supercalifragilizedwolverines" may impress, but believe me, your message will die right there on your front lawn.

- **Focus on what you do, not how you got there.** In my (former) corporate life, it mattered how I got to my current position; history was tied to credibility. When I went off on my own however, I (slowly) realized that nobody cares. All they want to know is what you do and how it can help solve a problem (today).

- **Keep it short.** Last week I made the mistake of asking somebody what his company specializes in. After prefacing his answer with, "In a nutshell..." (a red flag for lack of brevity if ever there was one), he spent the next 20 minutes answering my simple question. Even if I understood and remembered the gist of what he said (I didn't), it was just too much for me to hold onto.

By the way, in case you're wondering what I e-mailed back to that boy's mother, here it is:

"I'm a marketing consultant, and I specialize in electronic newsletters for professional services companies (attorneys, financial planners, executive recruiters, etc.). You know how everybody wants more clients? What I do is help professionals create informative, non-salesy newsletters they can send to their house list of contacts. As a result, they stay top of mind, and when somebody has a need that they can fill, the phone rings."

It's not poetry, I admit, but her reply back to me — "Got it." — was all I was looking for.

Lesson #12

Figure Out What Your Clients Value in You

It was February of 1980, and my friend Rob and I were sitting in the lobby of the School of Education at McGill University in Montreal. We were second-year students at the time and quite pleased with ourselves in the face of Rob's most recent discovery.

The simple truth that Rob had uncovered was this: The School of Education is *overwhelming* dominated by female students. You can walk the halls, sit in the lounge, read in the library, whatever. Everywhere you look, there are ten women for every man. If ever there were a place worth hanging out in, this was it.

And so we sat there in the lobby on that chilly winter night, quietly discussing an attractive woman across the way.

Suddenly, without warning, she slammed her book closed, jumped up out of her seat, pointed one of her fingers (I believe it was the middle one) in our direction and stormed away.

Needless to say, we were shocked. What we couldn't understand was how somebody sitting *way* on the other side of a big, open area could possibly have heard what we were saying. Could it be, as Rob suggested, that she was both beautiful *AND* the possessor of superhuman hearing?

No, as it turned out, the answer was much more mundane. It seems Rob and I both had head colds that day, and (we later realized) both of us were having trouble hearing. According to eyewitnesses, Rob and I were nearly shouting our conversation that night, even though the two of us *thought* we had only been whispering.

By the same token, it's not uncommon for the people *inside* an organization (even an organization of one) to have a distorted view of how it's perceived by the outside world. For example, you may be proud of certain company characteristics which clients hardly notice and you may be overlooking or downplaying traits that are highly valued.

Why does this matter? I'm so glad you asked.

It matters because to the extent your marketing materials—your web site, your newsletter, your business cards, your *words*—are an effective tool for attracting clients who like the way you talk, think, behave and operate, you've got to make sure that they *reflect* these highly valued characteristics. And unless you know what these things are, you can't deliberately bake them into everything you do.

With that in mind, here's what I recommend: Send an e-mail to (at least) 15 people who know you well. Choose a mix of friends, clients, colleagues, relatives, etc. Tell them you're launching/revamping your business and want to know "the first three words that come to mind when you think of me or my company."

If you do as I suggest, three things will happen:

- **The responses will be extremely positive.** Short of attending your own funeral, this is about as good as it gets in terms of praise from others, so prepare yourself to enjoy this exercise.

- **The responses will be very similar to each other.** People who know you well, even if they occupy different corners of your business or personal life, tend to enjoy the same things about you.

- **The responses may seem unimportant from a business perspective.** What I mean is that many of the comments (e.g. "detail oriented," "reliable," "down to earth," "creative") may strike you as nice but not relevant. On the contrary, these are the ones to pay special attention to.

  Because while you may *believe* that clients hire you due to your fancy law degree or superior accounting skills, it's simply not the case. They can't judge your technical capabilities; they just assume they exist. What they *can* judge, and what they do care about, however, are the human traits of you and your organization. This combination of things is what makes you *you* and, frankly, what makes your firm different from the dozens of others which claim to offer similar services.

The best marketing is "attraction based" and works on a simple principle: Show the world what you're all about, so that those who like what they see can "recognize" you and step forward. If you can do that, you'll save yourself a ton of time, effort and marketing expense. You may even avoid a few middle fingers pointed in your direction.

Lesson #13

Take Full Advantage of Your Existing Relationships

I play basketball every Monday night in my town's middle school gym. It's always a fun time, and although the gap between my age and that of the average player seems to grow exponentially with each passing week, I don't mind telling you it's one of the things I look forward to most during the winter.

It doesn't come without a cost, however. Within minutes of leaving the gym, various parts of my body begin to stiffen up and hurt: my knee, my neck, my lower back, you name it. By the time I get home, I'm walking up the front steps looking like Fred Sanford (if you don't know who Fred Sanford was, you may be too young to be starting your own business).

I go inside, eat dinner, take a few Advil. Then I go upstairs and get in the bath for about 30 minutes, or until my wife Linda yells through the door, "You're not sleeping in there again, are you?!" The next morning, assuming I have not died, I get up and limp off to my office.

In between those fun but difficult Monday nights, I go swimming. Swimming differs from basketball in two important ways. First of all, when I swim I rarely come in physical contact with either the "playing field" or the other participants. Second—and I think this is related to the first point just mentioned—nothing hurts when I'm done swimming. In fact, rather than hobbling out of the gym as I do on Monday nights, I bound out the door of the YMCA pool feeling much better than when I came in.

The interesting thing is that both activities, basketball and swimming, give me exercise. We could argue over which is more effective in this respect, but I think you'd agree they are both reasonable paths towards physical fitness.

When it comes to growing your business (i.e. getting more clients), you've also got several reasonable options at your disposal. And, just as with basketball and swimming, some of these are more painful than others.

The most common approach among professionals looking for work is to target potential buyers of your service, find ways to get in front of them and convince them to hire you. Into this category fall such tactics as newspaper advertising, sponsorships, direct mail and (brace yourself) cold calling. All reasonable, all proven.

In my opinion, however, this "chasing strangers" strategy is the "Monday night basketball" equivalent of growing a professional services business. Because while it may get you to your goal, it's hard work, often painful and the longer you do it, the more you begin to wonder if maybe you're getting too old to be banging up against a bunch of people half your age.

Another option—the one which, as far as I'm concerned, is a lot more like swimming—is to worry less about the strangers and spend more of your time and effort cultivating the relationships you've already got. In other words, instead of constantly trying to expand your reach, focus your attention on strengthening connections with the people you already know.

After all, if you've been walking the Earth for 40+ years, you've probably got hundreds (thousands?) of names in your rolodex. Shouldn't you be leveraging these relationships?

Not only that, if like most professionals, you've discovered that referrals and word-of-mouth bring you the best clients, wouldn't it make sense to shake the relationship tree more systematically and more often, *before* you look for ways to increase your circle of prospects?

Dedicate yourself to maximizing your firm's most valuable asset: the people you already know. Cultivating existing relationships can get you just as much business as continually trying to identify and meet new people. As far as I'm concerned, it's a much more enjoyable way to get and keep your business in shape.

Lesson #14

Separate Useful Information From Self-promotion

A few years ago, at the conclusion of my son Jonathan's last year of preschool, we inherited the school's pet box turtle. We weren't in the market for a turtle mind you, but the school had been told in no uncertain terms by the Commonwealth of Massachusetts that the creature had to go.

Apparently, and on what I can only imagine was one hell of a slow day on the floor of the Senate, the State had determined that turtles are potential carriers of salmonella. Combining this discovery with the fact that the mean time between hand washing events for the average four-year-old is approximately forever, it was decreed that no preschool could house one of these animals on the premises. And so, in need of a home, Franklin the Box Turtle came along with us.

After determining that Franklin was, in fact, female (don't ask), we renamed her Frankie and found her a cozy place in the family room. Bearing in mind what the State had discovered, we instituted our own set of Frankie-care regulations. I'm happy to share them with you now:

- If you play with Frankie or touch her in any way, you must wash your hands (with soap) when finished.
- When feeding her, use one hand to open her cage and remove her food dish, and *the other hand*

to open the bag of lettuce in the refrigerator. Whatever you do, don't mix the two hands up.

Believe it or not, when it comes to the art of promoting yourself by giving away free information, you've got a similar challenge. Because while giving away useful, free, no-strings-attached information regarding whatever it is you specialize in is a fantastic way to develop a following and establish yourself as an expert, it's important *not* to mix this information with a come-on for your service. Doing so creates a number of problems:

- **It causes salmonella.** Ha, ha! No, actually, problem #1 is that it calls into question the validity of the information you provide and, by association, your standing as expert. If you've ever read a "white paper" where a company—in a supposed attempt to shed light on a given issue— continually concludes that its solution is the best one out there, you know what I'm talking about. Even if the points raised are true, the reader can't help but wonder what's *not* being said.

- **It cuts down on information sharing.** Good information gets passed around—to friends, colleagues, clients and anyone else a recipient thinks might benefit. When that happens, not only does it raise your stature among those who've requested your information, it exposes you to their circle of contacts. That's good, that's exciting, that's what viral marketing is all about— other people doing your marketing for you.

But people don't forward advertisements; they share information because they think it has value. And every step you take in the direction of polluting your purely useful content (in the mistaken belief that by sneaking in your name more often you will somehow increase your brand value) lessens the likelihood that recipients will share your words with others.

- **It drops you back into the pack with everybody else.** Much of what's out there today under the heading of "marketing and advertising" is deliberately misleading. Ice cream containers in the supermarket are surreptitiously redesigned into smaller sizes, so that we don't notice the associated (per ounce) price increase. Companies claim, "Nobody offers better service than we do," which is really just an upside-down way of saying, "We all offer the same service."

  When you and I, on the other hand, give away unbiased, useful information, we stand out. We've all become so accustomed to waiting for the other shoe to drop that when it doesn't, not only will people believe what you have to say, they'll come knocking on your door when they have a need you can satisfy.

It's fine and important to promote your business and yourself as a solo professional. Don't make the mistake, however, of turning your "information pieces" into thinly disguised promotions. Include your name, copyright and company information (so those who receive it can find their way back to you), but if you label it as "unbiased information" (or white paper or FAQ or industry brief), keep the content itself as clean as a freshly washed pair of hands.

Lesson #15

Quickly Get the Attention of Your Audience

When we were fresh out of college, my friend Tom told me his theory about picking up women: The better-looking you are, the more *time* you have to make a good impression on a stranger.

If you're average-looking, Tom concluded, you have about two minutes. A little better than average, a little more time. A little worse than average, a little less time. In my case, unfortunately, this worked out to *negative* time, which essentially meant that I had to make a good impression on a woman about 30 seconds before I arrived.

In any case, while I'm not sure about the numerical accuracy of Tom's conclusions, I do think he had a valid point in general: First impressions matter, and the more intriguing something is at the beginning—*for whatever reason*—the more willing we are to give it a chance to prove itself.

Consider for example, the opening sentence of the book *Free Agent Nation* by Dan Pink: "I suppose I realized that I ought to consider another line of work when I nearly puked on the Vice President of the United States."

I don't know about you, but I would find it practically *impossible* to read a sentence like this and not continue. It's so intriguing and so seemingly out of context that you can't help but wonder what comes next.

Which is why I spend more time on the opening sentence of each newsletter, presentation or article I write than on any other part of the entire piece. Given that from the point of view of a member of my audience, the cost of deleting or ignoring what I've got to say is nearly zero, I'm very conscious of pulling him or her in right from the start.

Some examples:

(From a newsletter) "If you ask me, winter in New England (like pregnancy) is about a month too long."

(From a presentation) "I don't know if you've ever had a loaded gun pointed at you, but it's happened to me twice."

Nothing earth-shattering here, I admit. Still, I think you'd agree that both of these openings are unusual enough and intriguing enough to grab your attention and give you a reason to stay tuned for more.

And that, in a nutshell, is the key to starting your communications. Rather than slowly warming up to the good stuff, find a way to pull people in right from the beginning.

After all, most information-oriented communications — whether speeches, articles, memos, newsletters or whatever — begin exactly as you'd expect: on point and on topic.

There's nothing particularly *wrong* with that approach, but there's nothing particularly captivating about it either. And in a world as busy and cluttered with options as ours, captivating is what it's all about.

Now if only Tom and I had realized that 25 years ago.

Lesson #16

Seek Visibility; Forget About Theft

According to my friends at the Reference Desk of the Boston Public Library, the U.S. retail industry lost $13 billion in 2006 as a direct result of shoplifting. That's right, a staggering thirty-five million dollars *a day* walks right out the door.

Wouldn't it be great if there were an easy way to put an end to all this? Well, with that in mind, I'm happy to report that I've come up with a simple solution: Strip search all shoppers as they leave the store.

Think about it: Every person, every store, every day, retailers around the country enlist an army of people to search shoppers for stolen merchandise. Instead of hiring greeters to shake your hand as you come in, Wal-Mart would hire *gropers* to shake everything else as you leave.

Okay, put down your stolen merchandise and raise your hand if you think this is the dumbest idea you've ever heard. Me, too.

The problem, of course, is that the solution—while certainly helping on the stolen merchandise side of the equation—would have an even greater, negative impact on the sales side. Few people would submit to this type of harassment, and whatever a store gained in reducing theft it would lose many times over in lost sales.

By the same token, there's an orientation among many of us in the professional services world to overprotect (in my opinion) our intellectual property. In other words, while

I fully support the idea of placing an explicit copyright on your work as you produce it (something as simple as "Copyright 2007, Michael Katz. All rights reserved." will do the trick), many people take it a painful step further by adding all kinds of onerous legal text, in which they warn others not to reprint, reuse, redistribute or even think about the contents of whatever information they've just received (whether free or paid for). Similarly, many web sites that house this content impose technical barriers—password protection, randomly generated URLs, unprintable PDFs, etc.—which, while certainly making the content more secure, also makes it more inconvenient for legitimate purchasers to download and manage.

Personally, this doesn't make much sense to me. Because while I appreciate your interest in preventing others from stealing your original thoughts and words, the point of creating information in the first place is for others to get their hands on it. In other words, you've got a lot more to gain by letting the "good customers" get your information easily than you have to lose by guarding against the few (and they are few) who want to steal or misuse it.

The fact is, if your content is well done, and you offer it in a digital format, sooner or later somebody is going to steal it. For those people, all the scary language and technical inconveniences that you put in the way aren't going to make a difference. Instead, do as any successful retailer does and write off that kind of theft as simply the cost of doing business. Then focus your attention on helping the world to get their hands on your wisdom.

Lesson #17

Beware of Successful People

I attended an evening business event recently, primarily because one of the featured speakers was my friend and fellow consultant, Steve. (Not his real name. His real name is Nick Miller. I'm calling him "Steve" to protect his anonymity.)

Anyway, I went to see "Steve," and as always, he was impressive. I've seen him speak several times over the last few years, and every time I do, I walk out of the room newly energized and eager to jump back into my own work.

It wasn't always like that, though. In fact, I remember the very first time I saw Steve speak. It was February of 2001, and again, Steve was the featured speaker, and I was sitting in the audience.

I hung on every word, and I drove home that night with two very clear thoughts bouncing around inside my head:

- **I want to be that guy.** A confident, successful, solo professional, who had the audience laughing, learning and benefiting from his point of view. Watching Steve gave me my first clear vision of what I wanted to become as the owner of my own business.

- **I'm in big trouble.** The problem was that although I admired Steve, listening to him describe his systematic, targeted, "losing is not an option" approach to identifying and winning clients gave me a distinctly sick feeling in my stomach. I wanted what he had, but the thought of doing what he did to get it made me queasy. I'm not a good planner; I thrive on randomness. I don't like calling people I don't know; Steve's approach seemed to involve a lot of this. I prefer working with small companies; Steve's clients were the 50 largest banks in the country. And on and on and on. By the time I pulled into my driveway 30 minutes later, I was well beyond self doubt and now simply hoping that "extreme naiveté" would be considered a legitimate enough mental illness for my disability insurance to kick in.

Today, six-plus years later, I'm happy to say that seeing Steve hardly ever makes me feel sick. And here's why: I've realized that there are several ways for each of us to get to wherever it is we want to go. What works for Steve (or any other visibly successful person) is not necessarily (or probably) what's going to work for you or for me.

The problem with listening to experts—whether a thriving solo professional or a world-famous Fortune 500 CEO—is that the really good ones leave you with the distinct impression that they've "found the path." They're very clear about how they do what they do and why it works, and they have all kinds of real world experience with which to back it up. And if you're in the early stages of developing your own approach (as I was back then), with no evidence to the contrary, it's natural—no, intelligent—to copy somebody who's been there.

Or maybe not. Because what I've discovered as I've listened to Steve and many other successful people talk about "what works" is that what they're really talking about is what works *for them in particular*—given who they are, how they view the world and what they're naturally good at. For me and Steve, the answers to those questions couldn't be more different.

As far as I can tell, "success" (however you define it) is much more a function of knowing what works for you than knowing what works in general. And so while I strongly recommend listening, reading, watching and learning from as many experts as possible, don't let anybody else's "proven method" for reaching the top divert you from whatever path you're already on. If somebody else's advice strikes you as off-target, it probably is (for you).

Lesson #18

Say "No" to the Wrong Clients

I got a call a few months ago from Dan, a man in Atlanta whose company develops "perimeter security devices." I know, I had no idea what those were either, but Dan and I hit it off right away, so we kept talking.

We saw eye-to-eye on the topic of relationship marketing, and it wasn't long before he asked if I'd be interested in writing detailed product descriptions for his two dozen products. It seemed a reasonable fit for my skills, so I told him I'd take a look at his web site and get back to him with a proposal.

Unfortunately, I just couldn't seem to get interested. I really liked Dan, but the subject matter and particulars of the project just didn't grab me. A few weeks later, after struggling with it for several days, I called him and said, "You know what, this just isn't for me."

To Dan's credit, he was as nice as could be (which gave me pause yet again), and after agreeing to get together if we were ever in the same city, we went our separate ways.

Here's the point: Turning down business from nice people with plenty of money, simply because the work doesn't interest you, may seem to be a luxury that only well-established, overbooked professionals can afford.

It's not. In fact, in my experience, turning down the "wrong" work is the path to becoming a well-established and overbooked professional. Here's why:

- **When you do work you love, it's easier to do.** I've got some newsletter clients I've been working with for over five years. In each case, I'm as eager to work with them on their newsletters as I was when we first got started.

  The thrill of gaining a new client dissipates quickly, and even if the money is good, when the smoke clears, what you're left with is the work to be done. If you don't enjoy that, it will soon become a burden, making everything you do harder.

- **When you do work you love, you do a better job.** I'm happy to say that most of the things I write for clients are accepted with a minimum of changes, and I can't remember the last time I was asked to completely redo something.

  Guess what? It's not because I'm brilliant (although I am good looking). It's because there's such a good match between me, my clients and the work I've agreed to do, that the end result is nearly always on target.

- **When you do work you love, you attract more of it.** Actually, when you do *anything*, you attract more of it. Word-of-mouth means that clients tell others about completed projects, and if they liked it and you (even though you may have secretly hated every minute), their friends and others will start calling. Uh-oh, the "wrong work" is multiplying.

  Focus on what you love, on the other hand, and you're now moving in the right direction, with happy clients spreading the word and bringing more of what you want.

- **When you do work you love, you're not doing work you don't.** There are only so many hours in the day, and freedom to choose is one of the fortunate byproducts of working as an entrepreneur. You may as well have fun doing whatever it is you do (otherwise, it's called a job). When you walk away from the things that don't fit, you leave room for the things that do.

"Wrong clients" aren't bad, they (or the work) just aren't right for you. Part of your challenge, therefore, is figuring out which projects to steer clear of.

Easier said than done, I know. Particularly if you're just starting out, or if you don't have all the work you need, it may seem illogical, even irresponsible, to turn anything down. Believe me, I know the feeling.

I also know that the fastest, easiest and most enjoyable way to get where you want to be is to continually add interesting project on top of interesting project, and to walk away from things that are just "pretty good."

Lesson #19

Make Yourself Accessible

Lately, my wife Linda and I have been thinking about doing some home improvements. So the other day, I picked up the phone and called my friends over at Bank of America, to see about getting a home equity line of credit.

I pressed "1" to let them know I spoke English and "3" to let them know I wanted a home equity loan. I heard a few beeps, and then the following message: "All representatives are busy; please try back again later."

Huh? I've called places and been told they were not open. And I've certainly called places and been told they were busy, but please hang on. But I have to say this was the first time I'd ever been told—by the second largest bank in the United States, thank you very much—that my estimated on-hold time was approximately forever.

Now the truth is, I'm not telling you this story from the perspective of "customer service stinks and nobody cares anymore." No, that's not my message at all.

I've worked in and with enough large companies to know that the people responsible for managing inbound phone traffic are neither stupid nor uncaring. In fact, in my experience, it's just the opposite. Lots of very smart people in very large call centers around the world spend their working lives agonizing (yes, agonizing) over how to make your experience as a customer better.

The problem is, it's just not an easy nut to crack. Between staffing shortages, upselling targets, government regulations and the requirement of matching a particular caller's needs to the skill set of a particular agent (in real time, no less), it's a miracle that anyone can ever help you with anything.

That's life in a large company call center. Lots of calls, lots of employees, lots of training and lots of turnover. Lots and lots and lots of things that make it difficult to get the job done well, despite the best intentions of everybody involved.

You and I, on the other hand, don't have this problem; as small business owners, it's easy to provide great phone support. And when we do, we differentiate ourselves from our larger competitors who, mostly for reasons of size alone, can't get out of their own way.

Which is why I'm amazed when I see the walls that my fellow small business owners build between themselves and the outside world. Rather than trading on their natural, bureaucracy-free advantage, they accidentally (and sometimes deliberately) make themselves inaccessible.

And so with that in mind, I offer a few recommendations:

- **Answer your own phone.** I know you're busy and won't always be available, but if you're sitting there and the phone rings, pick it up. I know one consultant who never, *ever* answers the phone, preferring instead to screen every call and only returning those messages he deems worthy. If you want to develop a reputation as someone who's unreachable, this is a good way to do it.

- **Record a voicemail message with some life to it.** Telling callers "I'm either on the phone or away from my desk" is the voicemail message equivalent of "Have a nice day." It may have once served a purpose, but at this point it's become so clichéd as to be meaningless. Show callers there are actual human beings inside your company by saying something genuine and friendly.

• **Give callers an alternative way to reach you.** I provide a pager number as part of my voicemail message, so that those who really need to get a hold of me can give it a try. It's not 100%, but it's a second option that often does the trick.

• **Give clients your home phone number.** I know, I know, what if they call in the middle of the night? They won't. In seven years of giving my home number to every single one of my clients, I've gotten maybe two calls at home, and that was only after practically begging them to call me if there were some kind of emergency. This is a great example of a service feature that costs me nothing, but which is extremely valuable to a client who simply wants the peace of mind that comes with knowing that I'm reachable.

In a world filled with endless busy signals, on-hold messages, unreturned voicemails and "please hold while I transfer you" disconnections, you have an opportunity to solidify relationships with clients and others that can't be matched by your larger competitors—and it won't cost you a dime. Develop a reputation as an accessible individual, and always remember: some of those people are trying to give you their money.

Lesson #20

Learn to Tell Compelling Stories

We sold our house recently and moved across town. We weren't really looking, but something fell into our laps and we decided to jump.

It had been four years since our last move, and during that time, it was amazing to see how much the real estate industry had transformed itself. Thanks in no small part to the Internet, finding a home had become an easy, efficient, almost entirely online process, where buyers and sellers are perfectly matched in a fraction of the time it once took.

Ha, ha! Of course I am totally kidding. The fact is, nothing much had changed in those four years. Sure, buyers can now search for homes on the web at places like Realtor. com, but the descriptions are vague, the pictures are small and the goal of these sites is (as it always has been) to get you to pick up the phone and call a broker.

And that, I realized, is what had been bothering me. There I was, sitting on a house and property that I knew had many terrific, interesting, not-so-obvious qualities, and yet to any potential home buyer, these features were completely hidden by the established approach to marketing a home (i.e. six tiny photos and a one-paragraph description).

In other words, I knew that many of the people who would walk in the door would like what they saw, but how could I break through the clutter and get them in the door in the first place? If this sounds a lot like the dilemma you face every day in marketing yourself, stick around—I've got some suggestions.

After describing the situation to my friend Howie Jacobson, one of the most insightful direct marketers I've ever met (he's so insightful, he doesn't even do direct marketing for a living any more), he suggested I build a web site. A web site which told the story of my house in a personal, authentic, more-than-just-how-many-bedrooms-and-bathrooms-does-it-have kind of way.

I thought it was a terrific idea, so one day I sat down and did just that. When I was done, I realized one very important thing, a thing which completely relates to how you as a professional market your business:

Forget the features, spend time telling stories. I'm not saying features don't matter, but if everybody has the same ones, features quickly fade into the background.

Take a look at this. Here's an excerpt from the one-paragraph description of my house on Realtor.com:

> "The cabinet-packed cherry eat-in kitchen has
> a bay window overlooking a level back yard with
> a large deck and screened porch nearby."

Not bad, until you read an excerpt from another, similarly-priced house in our same town:

> "The home features a cabinet-packed kitchen,
> hardwood flooring, open floor plan, good sized
> bedrooms, master suite with bonus room and
> fireplace and finished lower level."

And another:

"Upgraded woodwork & moldings, cherry kitchen w/granite counters, hardwood floors on all 1st floor."

Frankly, I could hardly pick my own house out of the mix, since all the descriptions used the same tone and nearly the same words. If I'm having trouble, how could I expect to attract the perfect home buyer?

Similarly, when you describe yourself with overused words and phrases like "conscientious," "dedicated," "committed to excellence," "offering personalized service," etc., you sound like all the others.

Stories on the other hand, have two important things going for them:

- **Stories add warm flesh to the dry bones that are features.** A disgusting metaphor, I admit, but accurate all the same.

  It's one thing for me to tell you my property is 1.44 acres. It's something else entirely for me to show you a photo of my kids skating on a 70 x 30 foot ice rink in the front yard, accompanied by this snippet: "Sure, we could all skate across the street on the pond, but that's a three or four times a year event. As close as it is, it's still a hassle. My kids are out on our rink every single day, all winter long, and it's like a magnet for their friends (plan on going through a lot of hot chocolate)."

  Suddenly, 1.44 acres means something. You've got the same opportunity, every time you publish your newsletter, update your web site or introduce yourself to others. Start by showing pictures of real people in your firm, and get rid of those antiseptic stock photos of "businesspeople" looking vaguely constipated as they eagerly take in a PowerPoint presentation. Why hire models or buy images when you've got real, live human beings right there in your office? Hire a photographer (or do it yourself) to walk around your office with a camera for a couple of hours. Talk about real client projects in everyday language. Focus in on what you learned, as opposed to what you do. In essence, help readers (your prospects) smell the hot chocolate and hear the blades sliding over the ice. That's when they'll decide to hire you.

- **Stories are hard to steal.** One thing I noticed when I put my house on the market is that, at first blush, most homes seem to have the same stuff: bedrooms, basements, kitchens, decks, etc. I can use all the flowery adjectives I like to describe my particular stuff, but in general, all you hear is "blah, blah bathroom," "blah, blah screened porch."

  If, on the other hand, I tell you the story of my screened porch, and describe how I "dedicated an entire weekend to installing new screen wherever it was needed. I even spent half a day crawling around underneath the porch floor (yuck) with a staple gun in one hand and a roll of screen in the other, just to secure the floor from bugs," I own it. Nobody else can tell my story (authentically).

  Your experiences are similarly "unstealable." Nobody else can write about how you and your partner raised money for charity in a 5K run last year. Nobody else can talk about your dog who comes to work every day. Nobody else can explain how attending an overcrowded pool party last weekend reminded you of one of the principles of good market research.

You've got an endless supply of unique experiences—we all do—and by weaving them into your communications, you differentiate yourself from your equally skilled and equally qualified competitors.

Here's how the story ends. We sold our house—in the worst housing market in the Northeast in twenty years—to a couple who specifically told me (several times) how much the web site influenced their decision to come and see the house in the first place. When it comes to marketing professional services, personal stories told from real experiences will absolutely make the difference for you as well.

Lesson #21

Worry Less About Getting Good Press

Raise your hand if you remember what you were doing on the morning of March 4, 2001. No idea?

Okay, how about if I give you a hint: It was a Sunday. Still nothing?

Unlike you, I remember *exactly* what happened to me on the morning of Sunday, March 4, 2001. I woke up, went downstairs, opened the front door and picked up the *Boston Globe* off the front step. There, on the front page of the Business & Money section, was a huge article concerning small companies and their use of technology. But here's the best part: The first four paragraphs of that article were all about *me*.

Not incidental stuff either. Positive, specific, complimentary words about me and my business that positioned me as an expert and drew attention to my work. As my dad likes to say, "You couldn't pay for that kind of publicity."

I tell you this now for two reasons. Reason #1, to brag. Reason #2 (and much more relevant to your own success), to tell you about the *results* of that press coverage.

Here's what happened within the first week of the article coming out:

- Downloads of the free material offered on my web site went up by a factor of 65.
- Traffic to my web site went up by a factor of six.

- Sign ups to my newsletter went up by a factor of five.
- New clients for my consulting services went up by a factor of...well, not much.

As it turns out, I was able to track just *one* new client back to the publication of that glowing article: It was a guy I went to college with and hadn't spoken to in years. He saw the article, called to say hello and, as it turned out, he was in need of my services.

Think about that. The Sunday *Boston Globe* has a circulation of over 1,000,000 people, and out of all those readers, I gained just one client. I don't have my calculator handy, but I'd say that's roughly one in a million.

Compare that to the results I get from the publication of my twice-monthly E-Newsletter. As of this writing, it goes out to 5,500 people, and in a typical year, it brings me 25 new clients. One in a million versus one in 220.

Why such a difference? Two reasons: targeting and frequency.

- **Targeting.** The people I interact with every day — whether through my E-Newsletter, casual lunches, phone calls, cups of coffee, etc. — are people who have an interest in talking to me. Whether out of friendship, a need for information or an interest in growing their own business, everyone with whom I communicate is there on purpose.

  The *Globe*, on the other hand, goes to all of New England. And even though the starting point is one million people, when you account for all the people that didn't get around to reading the *Globe* that day, have no interest in business, or simply missed that particular article, I'd be surprised if there were even one thousand people left out of the initial pool of one million. Big numbers don't mean anything if nobody's paying attention.

- **Frequency.** It's thrilling to be featured prominently in the paper, but it's a one-time event. And no matter how impressed a potential client may have been at that moment, it doesn't add up to serious work. The fact is, anybody who hires a professional based on a single newspaper article is suspect.

  Contrast that with the people who evolve out of your ongoing relationships. These people come slowly, over time, and as the result (typically) of repeated interactions. For a professional, the best clients are those who take their time getting to you, and only appear after seeing or hearing about you several times.

Press coverage is great, but it ain't no marketing program. And while for most of us, "seeing my name in print" feels like the ultimate score, in practice, it's a lot less effective than simply devising ways to continually stay in touch with your house list (i.e. the people you already know). Find ways to make that happen, and you'll have a sales-generating machine even the *Boston Globe* can't match.

Lesson #22

Develop the Vision of Your Business

One of the interesting side effects of relying exclusively on E-Newsletters to market my business is that 100% of my prospective clients *reach out to me*, rather than vice versa.

In other words, instead of identifying industries or companies or individuals who seem to be the likely buyers of my services and trying to get in touch with *them* (the way most experts would advise), I simply publish a newsletter every other week, sit in my office drinking coffee, and wait for the phone to ring (what can I tell you, it seems to work).

As a result of this approach, and again, unlike the experience of most professionals, in that first conversation with a prospective client, I usually know absolutely nothing about who they are or what they do.

I know, I know, that's a cardinal sin in the world of sales. You're *supposed* to do all kinds of research regarding a prospective client and the industry it lives in before getting on the phone with them. How else can you impress them with your intimate knowledge of what they do and the problems they face, and avoid looking foolish and ill-informed during that first, all-important discussion?

Good question. You'll be pleased to know that I've developed and fine-tuned a Proprietary Interrogation Methodology™ (PIM), which allows me to learn all about a prospect *without* compromising my position as all-knowing consultant in the process.

And you'll be even more pleased to know that I'm going to share this entire blueprint with you, today, at no additional cost (you can thank me later).

It's tricky, though, so watch carefully. Here goes:

When I'm on the phone with a prospect, after exchanging the usual pleasantries and chitchat, I pause and take a deep breath. Then I look straight at the phone, and with a confident, yet inquisitive voice, I say: "So, what do you do anyway?"

Bam! That's it. They start talking and we're off and running.

All kidding aside, I have noticed one interesting thing in these situations. If the person on the other end of the telephone works as a "typical" professional (accountant, recruiter, financial planner, marketer, etc.), they answer my question by explaining their business model. For example, "We help mid-size technology companies market their products, using our five-point system for blah, blah. We zippity-zip their doo-dahs, and charge a licensing fee and hourly rate." You get the picture.

If, on the other hand, I ask this very same question to someone in a *nonprofit organization*, they invariably answer by explaining their vision. For example, "We help adults improve their economic situation by teaching literacy."

The nonprofit people never begin by talking about how they generate revenue. And, unlike their for-profit counterparts—who go as silent as if I had just asked them to explain how the Hubble Telescope works—they have no trouble talking coherently and at length about the "cause."

Why should they? The cause is what they do; it's why they come to work every day.

How about you? If thinking about the cause or vision or philosophy for your business makes you uneasy, you're in luck. Because if you've managed to sell what you do so far without even knowing what your cause is, you're going to love how much easier things get when you talk to people from a higher perspective.

What I've realized (and only recently) is that vision— not features, not benefits, not process, not capabilities, not credentials—is the fastest and easiest path to closing a sale. It is so much (sooooooo much) simpler to bring a new client onboard when they understand and buy into your "stuff." If your view of the world resonates with them and some problem they have or opportunity they see, they don't care (much) about how you get them there.

That last point is so important I'm going to say it again, in case you missed it: If they buy your vision, they don't care about your process. They just want you to take them to that place you just described.

In my case, during that critical, first impression conversation with prospective clients, I hardly talk at all about what I do (E-Newsletter creation). Instead, the vast majority of the discussion is about my vision: why relationships matter; how efficient it is to market to the people you already know; how difficult it is to chase strangers and position yourself as expert at the same time, etc. Vision, vision, vision.

A couple more things on this:

- **You don't need a "save the world" vision.** It's fine if you have one, but when I talk about vision, I'm simply talking about something bigger than just putting cash in your pocket. There's nothing wrong with cash, but if you want more of it with less effort, see if you can stand back and figure out what point of view your company has that transcends the money machine itself.

- **If you can talk about the vision independent of your particular service solution, you're on the right track.** Being able to clearly and concisely describe what you do and how you do it is certainly important. But that's not vision; that's just basic marketing. I'm talking about your view of the way things ought to be:

  Vision: "Small businesses deserve a way to inexpensively generate targeted leads"
  Service: Pay Per Click marketing from TakeAimSearch.com

  Vision: "Having a chronic illness doesn't mean you can't continue to thrive in the workplace."
  Service: Coaching from CICoach.com

  Vision: "Simplicity."
  Service: Web demos and presentations that connect instantly from Glance.net

  You get the idea. These visions exist *above and beyond* the services attached (in fact, you could apply the same vision to *other* services).

- **Take a lesson from the nonprofits.** In a nonprofit, the vision is always visible and right out there on the table. Nobody's there for the money, and everyone talks (constantly) about the cause.

Now, imagine for a moment that *your* business were set up as a nonprofit. Sorry, didn't mean to scare you. But what if money were not the objective? What would be the purpose of your organization? Chew on that one for a while and you may begin to see your vision!

Money's great (I like it a lot), but if that's the only reason your company exists, you're going to have to work for every sale. Talk less about what you do and more about what you believe, on the other hand, and you'll make it easier for prospects to hear you, understand you, remember you and (ta da!) hire you.

Lesson #23

Take Advantage of Being Local

Several years ago, the company I worked for was purchased by a telecom giant whose name I won't mention, other than to say that it kind of rhymed with "Hey Tea & Tea."

A few weeks after the announcement, we got word that the CEO of our new owner was coming to town to speak on a panel. Hoping to get a firsthand look at him, a bunch of us drove into Boston to see the event.

What can I say, he was impressive. Good-looking, well-dressed and articulate, he spoke about the future of technology as persuasively as a seasoned politician. Not only that, despite living a few thousand miles away, he peppered his talk with all kinds of local references—the Red Sox, The Big Dig, the cold weather, etc.

The fact is, he had the audience eating out of the palm of his hand. That is, until he made one critical mistake.

He mispronounced "Worcester," a city west of Boston. Instead of saying "Whuh-stah," as we natives have ridiculously agreed upon, he said "War-ches-ter." A reasonable assumption, but totally wrong.

Needless to say, the spell was instantly broken, and the next speaker on the panel—the CEO of a much smaller but local competitor—gleefully pronounced the word correctly when it came his turn to speak.

I mention this now because as a group, I often find that we solo professionals are much too eager to give away one of our greatest advantages relative to our national competitors: our local presence.

Afraid of appearing "too small," we try and look like the big guys and, in the process, ignore the fact that we live and work in the same communities as our clients and prospects.

The truth is, I don't fault my big company CEO friend for making the mistake he made. I give him credit for trying.

His problem, however—and the problem of any company that operates in many different locations—was in sounding real and genuine to the people on the ground (i.e. the customers). You can do all the research you want about a particular place, but from thousands of miles away, you'll miss the nuances. And missed nuances are what we locals notice immediately.

In terms of the way you talk about yourself and market your practice, the implication is clear for any professional who operates in a geographically limited area: *Stress* your localness and deliberately say and do things that your national competitors can't.

Can't, because they're either unaware of what's happening on the ground, or because they are constrained by the need for "location neutral" materials, promotions and messages that work anywhere.

Some specific examples:

- If you're a small financial planner who only works in Wisconsin, mention your recent trip to the Wisconsin State Fair in your next presentation.
- If you're a husband and wife executive recruiting team based in New York City, put a picture on your web site of the two of you standing in front of the Statue of Liberty.

- If you're an architect in Toronto, sprinkle your project portfolio with photos and mentions of local landmarks and neighborhoods.

There are many things to learn from big companies; operating a business from 30,000 feet isn't one of them. This top-down view of the world is a weakness, an organizational necessity for a group of people who are spread out all over the map. As a solo professional, it's the last thing you want to copy.

Lesson #24

Don't Ignore Your Flashes of Insight

It was July of 1993, and my son Evan was five months old. As any new parent knows, new babies require a lot of maintenance, and those first few months are exhausting.

The good news for my wife Linda and me was that, at five months, Evan was already sleeping through the night. The bad news, unfortunately, was that the night was only three hours long.

And so at around 5 a.m. on this particular Sunday morning, Evan was already awake for the day. I was sleepily doing laps with him downstairs, in the naive hope that he would eventually stop crying.

As I repeatedly passed our front door, I couldn't help but notice a small, red pickup truck parked in front of our house. This was odd, because with plenty of available parking on the street at *any* hour of the day, people tended to park in front of whatever house they were visiting (and there was nobody visiting us at the time).

A few Daddy-laps later, the morning's oddness score went off the charts. Here's what I witnessed out the front window:

A young man (maybe 18 years old) jogged up the hill towards our house, carrying a ladder. He gently put the ladder in the back of the pickup truck, climbed into the driver's seat and released the emergency brake. Without starting the engine, he coasted down the hill and out of sight.

I knew what I had seen, but even after thinking about it for several hours, I couldn't put the pieces together. Why did he have a ladder? Why didn't he start the engine? And, most importantly, who was he?

That afternoon, I paid a visit across the street to my neighbor John, hoping he might shed some light on the situation. To his credit, John figured it out in about 30 seconds. "Easy," he said, "I bet that was Cindy's boyfriend."

Suddenly, it all made sense. Cindy was our then 17-year-old neighbor. The ladder was for the boyfriend to get to Cindy's second floor bedroom window. The coasting down the hill was to keep from waking Cindy's parents.

I'm a big fan of "flashes of insight." One minute, confusion; the next minute, all the pieces fall into place.

That said, and as any serious professional will tell you, you can't rely on flashes of insight to run a real company. Which, I realized in a flash of insight several years ago, is why I no longer work for a real company.

Some of the best (and most profitable) ideas I've had—naming my company Blue Penguin, publishing a free educational newsletter, deciding to build a business around E-Newsletters in the first place—seemed relatively irrational (okay, stupid) when I first had them.

What I found, however, is that sometimes you need to jump all the way in and do what seems right before you really know why, and *well* before it becomes apparent how the pieces fit together. Frankly, I consider this a competitive advantage for any solo professional.

In other words, since those of us who work solo don't have to explain—or even understand—our next move to a partner (or, God forbid, a room full of spreadsheet-plugging managers who keep interrupting the discussion with the phrase, "Let me play devil's advocate for a minute"), we can run with things that aren't yet fully baked.

That's big. Not every great idea makes sense *before* the fact (I still have trouble imagining how anybody ever persuaded a bank to install the first ATM: "All you do is fill the box with about $50,000 and then leave it on the street corner overnight."). If you wait until it does, you'll do more waiting than doing.

If you find this way of thinking intriguing, here are a few suggestions for incorporating more flashes of insight into the way you do business:

- **Do things you like doing.** I got started in E-Newsletters after writing my own twice a month for about a year—simply because I liked doing it. Eventually, people came to me asking for help with *their* newsletters. I wasn't in the E-Newsletter business at the time (there was no such thing in 2000), but one day it just hit me—I could do this for other people.

- **Do things that fascinate you, even if there is no obvious payback.** For example, I think audio is going to be big in the business world, so about a year ago I started podcasting my twice monthly newsletter. If there's a business model for me in there somewhere, I sure don't know what it is. That's fine with me. I'm getting involved *now*, under the assumption that my audio flash of insight will bear fruit down the line.

- **Do things before you know what you're doing.** When I started working with clients on their E-

Newsletters, I didn't really have a process. After weeks of thinking about it, talking about it and trying to figure out the "best way," I just waded in and (shhhhh) *made it up as I went along.* Guess what? Clients loved it, and the process that I now have was established after the fact (and still evolves to this day).

Lots of people (and most companies) need to "make the numbers work" before they're willing to invest time and money on a new idea. If that's the way you like to approach things, too, that's fine.

If it isn't, however, and like me, you feel the creative side of your brain shutting down when too much logic is applied, don't worry. I absolutely guarantee you that a less-structured approach to doing things works just as well.

Lesson #25

Stay In Touch With Past Clients

It seems that everybody's got a story about his or her own lousy experience interacting with a car dealer. Don't you wish that just once people would stop complaining, and say something positive for a change?

Me neither. Which is why I'd like to share *my* story. A couple of years ago, my wife Linda and I bought a new car, a Honda Odyssey minivan. It's a terrific vehicle, and despite my initial fears, I have to admit that even the buying process itself was flawless—a textbook example of what good customer service ought to be.

The dealer was courteous and dependable, and in the end he even delivered the car to our house, despite the fact that we live a good 20 miles away. Not only that, but over the past two years, guess how many follow-up communications we've received regarding our vehicle?

If you guessed "zero," you are today's lucky winner.

Think about this. Linda and I decide to plunk down $20,000+, and not only do we get a great car, we are pleasantly surprised with a buying experience that is second-to-none. From a marketing perspective, the dealer's hard work is done. We know who he is, we like the way he does business, we feel well taken care of. There's no reason that we would ever go elsewhere.

Well okay, there is one reason. We don't like being ignored.

Because instead of staying in touch with us periodically—sending us a thank you note; sending us a follow-up survey; sending us monthly tips on caring for our vehicle; sending us a coupon for a free oil change; sending us an ice scraper with his name on it; inviting us to an open house to view next year's models, and on and on and on—he does nothing.

Instead, I watch week after week as he buys full-page ads in the Sunday paper, trying to entice perfect strangers into his showroom. I don't know, maybe he figures that out of a family of five—one of whom, I shudder to mention, is a mere three years away from getting his own license—none of us will *ever again* need to purchase a vehicle.

But hang on just a minute. Because before we spend any more time laughing at the size of his missed opportunity, let me ask you a question: What do *you* do to systematically stay in touch with the people who have bought something from you?

I'm going to guess from the awkward silence that the answer is nothing (sorry, sending invoices doesn't count). People hold out their money, you take it and you deliver a great service. But as soon as that's done, you're on to the next stranger.

I have news for you: most businesses don't need more customers. They just need more repeat business from the people who already know them. It is just so so so much much much easier to sell things to people who have already taken the hardest step of all: Giving you their money for the *first* time.

But they're not going to remember you; you need to remember them. And with that in mind, I offer three inexpensive, low-tech suggestions for getting you on your way:

- **Send a thank you note when somebody becomes a new customer.** If your business is the low-volume kind, handwrite it and send it snail mail.

- **Send a follow-up letter or e-mail 30 days later** asking for their feedback on how the buying process went, and whether or not what you sold them has been helpful/useful/valuable.

- **Send a thank you note (or even better, a gift)** one year after they make that first purchase.

Sure, you could do a lot more than just these three things to systematically stay in touch with your clients. But I guarantee you that these alone will speed you well ahead of your asleep-at-the-wheel competitors.

Lesson #26

Don't Argue With Your Clients

My friend Betsy and I got together for lunch the other day at a Japanese restaurant near her office. She'd taken me there once before, and I was looking forward to experiencing another terrific sushi lunch.

We sat down, ordered our food and continued our conversation. A few minutes later, the waitress arrived with lunch.

Mine was fine, exactly what I ordered. Betsy's, however, was wrong; the waitress had brought her something different by mistake.

That's when the fun began. The waitress wouldn't "allow" Betsy to exchange the order, insisting instead that she brought exactly what had been requested. As the conversation got more animated (and now fearing for the life of our waitress), I glanced over Betsy's shoulder and was relieved to see the manager making his way toward our table to intervene.

Hang on, it gets worse. To my utter amazement, the manager *also* insisted that the order had been taken correctly, explaining that he had overheard Betsy's request while cleaning up a neighboring table a few minutes earlier and that she was, in fact, in the wrong.

So here's my question for you: Who would you guess was right about the food order, Betsy or the waitress?

Here's my answer: It doesn't matter. Even if Betsy had made the mistake—which is likely, since both the waitress and manager claimed to have heard something different—there's nothing to be gained by proving a customer wrong. There is, however, plenty to be lost.

In this case, for less than a dollar's worth of food ingredients (the cost of throwing out the original order and bringing something else), that restaurant lost a loyal customer in Betsy; a once-in-a-while customer in me; and all of our combined future business from now until approximately the end of time. Talk about biting the hand that feeds you (or, in this case, that you're feeding).

The way I look at it, you've got two choices in your approach to handling clients: You can be right, or you can be rich. If you insist on winning arguments with your customers and clients, while you may enjoy the momentary satisfaction that comes with proving a point, you're going to spend a lot of time refilling your leaky (client) bucket.

If, on the other hand, you seek to solve problems from the perspective of making the lives of the people who give you their money easier, your clients will love you for it. Particularly the ones who already know (without your assistance) that the mistake was theirs.

Lesson #27

Tap Your Enthusiasm

"Enthusiasm is the inspiration of everything great.
Without it no man is to be feared, and with it none despised."
— Christian Nevell Bovee

I remember it like it was yesterday. It was my 43rd birthday, and I was outside the house, mowing the lawn and minding my own business. Suddenly, my wife Linda strolls up and says, "Honey, shut that thing off, we're going out tonight!"

I have to confess that at that point, just getting in the car and hiding around the corner long enough to miss the kids' bedtime would have sufficed as a birthday present, so when she pulled out two tickets to the hottest show of that summer, I was thrilled.

People say if you've never seen Bruce Springsteen live in concert, you've never seen a live concert. Based on what we experienced that night, I think there's a lot of truth to that. Here's a guy in his mid-fifties, jumping up on pianos, sliding across the stage on his knees (several times), going nonstop without a break for three solid hours, and by all indications, having at least as good a time as the 60,000 other people in the stadium with him.

The funny thing is, Springsteen's special talent—the one thing that distinguishes him from all the other equally-skilled guitarists, songwriters and vocalists—isn't a talent at all.

What makes him stand out from his peers is his enthusiasm. His ability to go out there year after year, long after he's stopped needing the money or the recognition, and perform every night like it's his first time—that's what puts him on the top of everybody's list.

You and I have the very same opportunity: Like Springsteen, we've got the skills necessary to get the job done (that's a given). What makes the difference, however, between huge success and a life (or business or career) of mere survival, is enthusiasm.

Yes, you need to have the fundamentals of your trade in place. But what I've come to realize is that the mechanics alone are not enough. Most of your competitors offer exactly the same basic stuff as you do; your enthusiasm is what will make the difference.

In my case, I love the idea of relationship marketing and E-Newsletters, and I never tire of talking about the subject (in fact, the more I talk about it, the more excited I get). Having switched careers from something I found vaguely interesting to something I'm legitimately excited about, I can tell you that it is infinitely easier to be effective when working on something that you love. (Do you think Bruce Springsteen enjoys rock-and-roll?) Not only that, but your "audience" can absolutely feel the difference.

The great thing about enthusiasm is that it's there for the taking. Anybody who wants it simply has to pick it up. And while it can't (completely) make up for a lack of skills, without it your business is destined to the middle of the pack.

Lesson #28

Work On Your Business, Not Just In Your Business

I have a confession to make. Sometimes when the weather is nice, in the middle of the week, I don't go into my office at all. I go for a bike ride in the woods, or to the beach with my wife, or I just take the train downtown and walk around.

Why am I telling you this? To emphasize the value of periodically stepping away from the work itself.

Here's what I mean. Although it may seem that there's a direct correlation between your effort and your financial compensation (and if you're a bill-by-the-hour professional, you may think you've got definitive proof), in practice, I think there's a lot more to it. In my experience, effort only gets you part of the way there (and it's the small part). The big leaps in profitability occur as a result of insights or refinements to your overall approach, and these big leaps are born when you step way back from the day-to-day.

Try this test: Think about your most profitable services or product offerings—the ones that really make a difference to your business. Where did they come from? Why and how did you create them? If you're like most of the professionals of whom I ask this question, your answer has something to do with gaining a new perspective on your business, *not with the implementation of details:*

"We decided to package up our knowledge into an audio tape series, and it just took off."

"We realized that we were selling to the wrong target group, and when we made the adjustment things got a whole lot easier."

"I decided to focus my business on the very narrow specialty of E-Newsletters rather than being a marketing consultant in general."

When I work with a company that's spinning its wheels—whether with respect to its E-Newsletter or with the marketing of the business overall—the answer never seems to show up in the details. It always boils up from the big questions: Who are you? What makes you different? What business are you in? Why would anybody want to do business with you in the first place?

The interesting thing about these significant adjustments in approach is that they aren't about working harder or smarter; in fact, they're not really about working at all. They're about seeing what you do and how you do it in a different way and from a different perspective.

In my case, those insights arrive through some combination of hot sun, reading things that have nothing to do with my work and literally wandering around. When I can manage to combine all three, I always return with a long list of big, new, fresh ideas for my business.

Bottom Line: Conventional business wisdom suggests that there's a high correlation between effort and financial success; the harder you work, the more money you make. And while I mostly agree with this in the context of a given workday or a given project, the big leaps don't come from running harder, or even running more efficiently. They come from stepping back periodically and making sure you're still running in the right direction.

P.S. If you work for yourself, although you have an unlimited amount of "theoretical free time," you may find it even harder to give yourself permission to take a day out of the office. Believe me, I know the feeling. I've learned, however, that when I view one of these days from the perspective of "making my business more enjoyable and more profitable"—rather than as *just* a vacation day—it's a lot easier to fit these into my calendar. See you in the sun!

Lesson #29

Take a Page From Michael Jordan

I made a mistake last week involving pants: I bought them. The problem is (and I have to say I pretty much knew this before I left the store), they don't fit.

In my defense, I am a man. I don't like clothes shopping to begin with, and when you throw in the extra step of having to try things on, I get to a point where I'd gladly plunk down my credit card on an ill-fitting clown suit if I thought it would get me out of the store faster.

But the real mistake was taking the pants home, cutting off the tags and *then* deciding they don't really fit. Now I'm stuck with them, and despite having spent the better part of this week trying to convince myself that they're okay, I know I am a liar.

In my experience (and in this case, I don't think it applies to just men), most of us settle on a profession in about the same way. We wander around, try a few things on, and if we find something we can squeeze into, we take it.

Unfortunately—I know based on e-mails, phone calls and cups of coffee with lots of working people—there are way too many of us just tolerating work, instead of thriving in it. We have, in effect, cut the tags off before finding a good fit.

Which brings me to Michael Jordan. Here's a guy who, in his 13 years as a professional basketball player, won just about every award imaginable in that sport; he's arguably the best ever to walk the face of the Earth. So much so that if you were to describe the attributes of the ideal basketball player, you'd more or less describe Jordan, up to and including his winning personality, which made him ideal for product endorsements.

But here's the key question: Was he really that extraordinary as a human being, or was he just lucky? Lucky, in the sense that the things that came naturally to him—height, speed, strength, intelligence, endurance, competitiveness and a love of basketball—just happened to be a perfect fit for an existing profession?

I believe it's more the latter. Sure he worked hard, but no more than you or I do. The fact is, if being unusually tall were a *negative* in basketball instead of the positive that it is, Jordan might have just turned out to be one more good-looking bald guy named Michael.

This next thing I'm about to say may sound like an exaggeration, but I don't think it is.

I think we're all Michael Jordans (or Oprah Winfreys or Donald Trumps, or anyone who's had extraordinary success in a given field). The problem is that for most people, the unique package of skills, abilities and interests within each of us doesn't fit perfectly and obviously into an existing profession. So we pick from among the available options and settle for "good enough."

Or maybe we don't. My view—after spending the first 20 years of my professional life in conventional jobs, being slightly successful doing things I slightly liked—is that the point of starting your own business is to create a custom-made occupation. A unique livelihood that pulls together all the things you love and are good at doing, into one basketball-dunking, crowd-pleasing, "Can I have your autograph, please?" concoction.

Why not spend a little less time straining to fit your idiosyncratic self into an existing pair of pants, and a little more time thinking about a new wardrobe entirely, one based on whatever natural talents and interests are uniquely yours? I'll see you at the All-Star game.

Final Thoughts

10 Really Good Reasons to Quit Your Job and Start Your Own Business

It's been seven years since I made the move to leave my corporate job and start my own company. No question about it, leaving nice coworkers, a stable paycheck and twelve years of tenure with one company was the scariest thing I'd ever done. And yet, looking back, it was the defining moment, not only of my career, but of my personal development as well. The fact is, I am now so enamored of blazing my own trail that I could never go back—I am hopelessly, incurably, unemployable.

As a result, I receive a steady stream of "Can I buy you a cup of coffee?" invitations—from old colleagues, new friends, complete strangers—anybody who is considering a change, and who wants to know, "Why should I start my own business?" This is what I say:

1. **You'll dance to your own music.** There's a lot of noise in the corporate world. Not physical noise, but opinions, rules, history and a whole lot of "that's the way we do it around here" always just an inch or two below the surface. In such a setting it's hard to find your path, or as I like to say, "hear your own music."

    Once you're on your own, you'll suddenly begin to hear what's there, and the more you can hear it and have the courage to follow it, the more enjoyable and, yes, profitable your life will be. The fact is, there is no right way to live, to act or to grow a business.

2. **You'll never have to retire.** Retiring is a strange concept to the satisfied, self-employed person. It implies that work is something you want to be done with, something you wish were over. When you truly find your passion, however, the concept becomes meaningless. Do painters stop painting? Do musicians stop playing music? Do comedians stop being funny just because they've reached a certain age? Not if they are doing what they truly want to be doing. Sure, you may slow down or change focus as you get older, but the game is never over, since the game and your life will be one.

3. **You'll put your money where your mouth is.** I never planned to start my own business, and I always secretly believed I didn't have the guts to be successful on my own. When I look back now, I'm not even sure how I managed to convince myself to leave the perceived safety of living within the protected walls of a large corporation. When I finally jumped, however, I was surprised by the number of friends, former co-workers and family who remarked on my "courage." Frankly, I'm not any braver now than I was before, but I know with certainty that I don't need a corporation to take care of me (and neither do you).

4. **You'll no longer live in two worlds.** I used to be two people: "corporate Michael" and "home life Michael." Corporate Michael was less friendly, less intuitive and a lot less interesting. I found it easy to switch back and forth between the two Michaels, and for a long time it didn't even strike me as odd that I would make decisions at work based on a completely different set of criteria regarding what was fair, what was smart or what was worth doing. That's over—I'm now one person no matter what I do, and I have a more balanced, more humanistic approach to business.

5. **You'll know your own power.** Swept up in the turmoil of working as part of a corporation, there's a tendency to blame others, wait for others, think that others are making things happen. Working alone, you'll realize how much control you actually have (and have always had). That realization will give you the courage and drive to do more things than you ever dreamed of back when you saw yourself as an insignificant part of a big machine. You'll have nobody else to blame, but even more importantly, you'll see how much credit you really do deserve for everything you've created.

6. **You'll be free to walk away.** When you first start out on your own, you will probably be grateful for whatever business comes your way. The thought of "walking away" from a client may seem suicidal. It isn't. As your reputation grows, people will approach you, ready to hand you their money and

have you begin work. That's terrific. However, in some cases, the fit won't be there; something in your gut will tell you it's a bad match. You will learn that you can say "No, thank you" and walk away. Nobody assigns projects or clients or teammates to you anymore. You and only you decide who you work with and on what terms, and if it doesn't feel right, you need only say so.

7.   **You'll make new friends.** If you've been with the same company for a long time, you've probably developed several close relationships. You may be afraid that you'll be lonely and isolated out here in the "cold, cruel world." Nothing could be further from the truth. Starting your own business gains you immediate entrance into a collegial world of fellow solo professionals and entrepreneurs, eager to have you along for the ride. We hold meetings, we have events, we meet for lunch, we talk on the phone. We share ideas, support each other and hang out together. Price of admission: a friendly demeanor and a willingness to help other people find their way.

8.   **You'll pick the players.** Wherever you sit in a company, you've got people you interact with every day: your boss, your direct reports, the head of the legal department, the desktop support guy, the receptionist. Hopefully you like and get along with most of these people, but whether you do or not, you're stuck with each other. When you run your own company, on the other hand, you pick who's on the team. You get to choose your

attorney, your accountant, your landlord, your partners, your clients—everybody in your daily life is there because you decided to put them there. You get to choose.

9.   **You'll have real problems, instead of imaginary ones.** In a corporate setting, your happiness and success are dependent upon dozens of intertwined relationships and handed-down decisions, any one of which can change your world in ways you may not anticipate or even understand. With so much out of your control, it's hard not to spend time "what if-ing" and worrying about the future. "What does my boss really think of me? What if I don't get put in charge of that new project? What if they cut my budget next year?" Fear of what might happen can become worse than the situation itself—imaginary problems.
When you're building your own business, you're immersed in reality. Sure, you may have days where you worry about paying the mortgage, but you'll be in the game, fighting the good fight, no longer obsessed with the possibility of being blindsided by an unforeseen shift in the corporate winds.

10. **You'll find your purpose.** You didn't come here to follow somebody else's vision or sit on the sidelines watching the clock tick away until retirement. But somehow, somewhere along the way, you forgot. Now, after so many years of following the pack, you've come to see work as a place you go to earn enough money to do the things you really want to do. It doesn't have to be that way. Working

on your own will give you the freedom and focus to find the exhilarating, balanced, self-directed career you've always dreamed of.

One of my favorite quotes is from the book *The Artist's Way*, and I've had it taped to the top of my computer monitor for the last seven years: "Leap, and the net will appear."

Go ahead, I'll be waiting for you.

About Michael J. Katz

An award-winning humorist, entrepreneur and recovering corporate marketer, Michael Katz translates his unique view of everyday life into useful, authentic and entertaining business insights.

As Founder and Chief Penguin of Blue Penguin Development, Inc., Michael is a recognized expert in the development of electronic newsletters, and helps clients significantly increase sales by showing them how to build on their existing relationships.

Since launching Blue Penguin in 2000, Michael has been quoted in The Wall Street Journal, The New York Times, Business Week Online, Bloomberg TV, The Boston Globe, The Boston Herald and other national and local media.

He is the author of three books, and has published over 175 issues of his "E-Newsletter on E-Newsletters," a biweekly with 5,000 passionate subscribers in over 40 countries around the world.

Michael has an MBA from Boston University and a BA in Psychology from McGill University in Montreal. He also has a second degree black belt in karate (Kempo), a first degree black belt in parenting (three children), and is a past winner of the New England Press Association award for "Best Humor Columnist."

Made in the USA
Charleston, SC
15 June 2013